JOY
in Ageing

JOY

in Ageing

POETRY COLLECTION

FOREWORD BY PAM RHODES

EMBRACING AGE
Later life in all its fullness

First published in 2024 by
Independent Publishing Network
Compilation © 2024 Embracing Age
Poems © individual poets
All rights reserved.

ISBN-13: 978-1-7395733-4-8

info@embracingage.org.uk

embracingage.org.uk

CONTENTS

FOREWORD BY PAM RHODES

One of my favourite hymns is that old childhood song, "Give me joy in my heart" – and when you're a child, there's so much in life to make you feel joyful! Family, friends, interests and talents shape a life that is full of experience and learning - and the more we know, the more possibilities open up to us, and the more enjoyable life can become.

But we're not children for long, and nowadays we live in such a fast-paced, demanding world, where the need to take responsibility, pay bills, keep a roof over our heads, and care for ourselves and probably a family too, can feel so relentless and competitive that "joy" is not a word that often comes to mind.

And by the time retirement looms, offering a chance for us to step off that treadmill of responsibility, we've probably blown out the candles on a lot of birthday cakes. And age has taken its toll, as wrinkles creep across our faces, our hair is thinner, our waistlines wider, our joints creakier, and we don't just run out of puff, we sometimes feel as if we have no puff at all. So, where's the joy in that?!

Well, joy bubbles through the wonderful collection of poems that were entered into our JOY IN AGEING competition! Whether the poets were in their fifties or their nineties, it was clear that, when it comes to thinking about whether their 'half-filled glass' is nearly empty or full, their lives are brimming over with contentment, pleasure and laughter in simple but significant ways.

And this comes from a generation who certainly have their own challenges to face. They acknowledge the physical toll on their bodies as years tick by – the things they shouldn't eat, the exercise they should be taking, and the pills that are lined to be swallowed three times a day. And, worst of all, the things they can't remember – the number of the bus that stops outside their garden gate; and the time they called their daughter three different names before they hit on the right one – and then the embarrassing realisation that those three names they came out with actually belonged to dearly-loved but long-departed family pets! But ask them what their Mum's old Co-op number was, or which one of the Beatles was their favourite, and their replies would be immediate and right on the button! And good memories, even if they aren't always complete or accurate, are clearly a huge source of joy in later life. How good it feels to recall happy times - wedding days, new babies, obstacles overcome, ambitions achieved, old friends and warm hugs – all part of a joyful treasure store of comfort and pleasure to savour once the world has become a little smaller, life a bit quieter, and an hour's nap after lunch is a highlight of the day!

One thing that struck me about these poems is how often friends and family are a source of great joy – whether it's sharing a quick cuppa with someone their own age, or the huge sense of pride and overwhelming love they feel not just for their children, but especially their grandchildren. Pets are often mentioned too, for the sheer joy of companionship and unconditional love they bring to later life. And could anything be more pleasurable, when you're out walking the dog, than choosing to sit a while on a park bench, taking in the intricacy and wonder of God's glorious creation all around us?

It HAS been a joy to see how pleasure and contentment can become the bedrock of our lives as we grow older. And through these poems, we see that love is often at the heart of that inner joy – the love that comes to us, the love we feel for others, and the love of God that blesses the length of our lives.

Autumn by Robin Salter
Winning Art Entry

Embracing Age

ALWAYS REVERT TO THE NAVY
ALI MITCHELL

You should always revert to the navy as the safest of
　　colours to choose
It's the shade with provision for every event and the
　　best on the spectrum of blues

There's a calm resignation in navy to a fate inescapable
　　too
Which appeals to the oldies amongst us, makes you
　　feel like you're part of the crew

When life's course has proved lengthy and stormy, as
　　good memories retract and then fade
And you're clinging to what provides safety, jump
　　aboard with the navy brigade

At least that's what Gran always told me and I always
　　believed what she said
But, a gran now myself, I'm rebelling (yet her words
　　echo still in my head)

Though I miss you, dear Gran, that's a given, and your
　　wisdom has mostly prevailed
When it comes down to navy and ageing, that old ship
　　well and truly has sailed

11

Joy in Ageing

Lovely Gran, you missed out on rebellion and were
    never allowed to let rip
But my mutinous will has determined to vow that I'm
    not going down with that ship

So I can't get on board with your wisdom, due to
    things that still haunt me from school
Like compulsory wearing of big navy pants, young or
    old those were clearly not cool

I rejoice in the colours of nature and delight in
    exploring what's new
With a spring in my step borne of freedom, now retired
    there's just so much to do

We old folks can now dress like the young ones
    without fear of chastisement or scorn
Outward signs of the soul's liberation like the joy felt
    from being reborn

Let free spirits join forces together never caring what
    others might think
As we strut down the street in our casual gear, denim
    trousers and hair glowing pink

So what else can I say about navy that has not yet
    already been said?

Embracing Age

Just that steering your own course through ageing
    always stands you in jolly good stead

Overboard with outdated traditions, being tarred with
    the age brush too soon
I'll revert back to navy when science disproves that
    marine tides are ruled by the moon

JUDGES' COMMENTS:

DAVE BILBROUGH WRITES:
It was Oscar Wilde, who is attributed to have remarked, 'Be yourself, everyone else is taken'. This poem by Ali Mitchell so wonderfully uses the metaphor of the uniformity of the colour navy, contrasting it with the possibilities of living with a wider palate of colour, boldness and adventure. Here lies a valuable lesson to us all. Growing older challenges us to rethink our perspective and to resist the fear of being out of step with others. Many of us tend to grow rigid and opinionated with age but Ali, through this poem, encourages us to be flexible and live life to the full.
This one got my vote for being both clever and original.

ANDREW PRATT WRITES:
When I first read 'Always revert to the navy' I was initially lulled into an expectation that I knew just where this was going. The poem was very well written, so that was good. It was enough to hold my attention and keep me reading. I was anticipating 'purple'. When someone has written such a familiar piece as 'When I am an old woman I shall wear purple', following in the same direction not only runs the risks of plagiarism and predictability, but of poor thought, lacking originality. The number of hymns I've been asked to critique that begin 'Love divine' or poems, 'I wandered lonely...' is legion. I was prepared for disappointment. Yet I read

on. You had caught me. I wanted to know how you would get yourself off the hook.

Then that line 'When it comes down to navy and ageing, that old ship well and truly has sailed...' caused an abrupt tack of direction, sailing into new waters and I found myself chuckling and physically guffawing. I was hooked on a text of originality and genius that could have sunk without trace. But even now the tides still turn and the moon still rules.

Thank you for this breath of fun and joy.

PAM RHODES WRITES:

Well done Alison - what a clever and witty reflection on how we're meant to behave throughout our lives, especially at the age when we're supposed to know better! Our hair may be thinner, our waistlines wider and our faces a roadmap of wrinkles – but inside I don't think we change much at all, however many birthdays we've had. We go through so many life stages in which we're expected to conform, from those navy knickers we hated to wear at school to the conservative business clothes we've probably worn for decades of work days. So, this witty poem that encourages us, in our most grown up years, to rebel against blandness and choose the freedom of flamboyance, is a breath of fresh air. Begone dull navy! I'm digging out my feather boa and a big red hat!

ABOUT THE POET

Ali

~~Amanda~~ is a retired administrator, having worked mostly in local newspapers and a national children's charity, alongside various other charity volunteer roles and many years of service as a deacon and church secretary in her former local family Baptist church.

She is blessed with two sons and one daughter. And a rescue cat. Until recently most of her life was lived in a village close to Haworth, so the Bronte sisters' remarkable literary legend was always fresh in her mind.

At college she studied modern European languages. She has a passion for language and loves playing with words. After retiring she began writing verse aimed at children and hopes one day to be able to publish.

Currently she facilitates her local library's writers group, where they encourage and inspire one another by sharing and discussing their individual written work.

NO RUSH (THE JOY OF BEING RETIRED)
DR RUTH EARDLEY (63)

A dying woman, too young at fifty-nine
And yet I was so conscious of the time.
(Afternoon surgery starts at three)
'I'm sorry to keep you here,' said she
She saw me glance at the watch on my sleeve
'If you could just sort out my pain relief.'

Medicine today is a ten minute quiz
With 'does it hurt here?' and 'can you feel this?'
And 'I'm sorry we can't really manage today
The six other things that you wanted to say.
I'll see you again. Please don't think me abrupt
But maybe the wait might just help it clear up!'

It was hard to retire from being a GP
Now nobody wants an opinion from me
I don't have appointments or thank yous or flowers
But I do have more energy, yes, and more hours
No management meetings or critical timing
But I guess that's the crux of this cloud's silver lining...

Now I don't leave the house and get back in the dark
I have time for that woman I met in the park
And out on the school run, my grandkids in tow,

Joy in Ageing

There's a young mum who chats and I know that she
    knows
That I'm happy to hear (since I'm not in a hurry),
That her baby's just fine but her sister's a worry.

And serving the juice at the church 'mums and tots'
I see so many people and find I learn lots
(Not least that the qualifications I need
Are to keep coffee flowing and top up the tea
And to chat with the carers and then to wash up)
And I think back to 'oldies' who poured me a cup.

So I'm happy and honoured to join in the ranks
Of the volunteers at the local food bank
And to be on the rotas and stack up the seats
And to visit the lonely old chap down the street.
Cos people need grannies - there's loads they can do
And when you're not looking, they pray for you too.

JUDGES' COMMENTS:

PAM RHODES WRITES:
Ruth has created a poem that touches me on so many different levels. How frustrating to become a GP because she cared enough to want to relieve the pain and fear of illness, only to find herself spending years on a treadmill where she always had to treat patients with one eye on the clock. In comparing her previous working life with her retirement, and the opportunities she has now to show care through volunteering, serving, chatting and even packing up chairs, Ruth reveals her real joy and contentment in conversation, hugs and the knowledge that when she asks her neighbour how they're feeling, she's got the time and compassion to REALLY want to know the answer.

And I love the last line – that whatever friendly or practical help she's able to give, she knows that a quiet prayer for someone in need will bring blessing and joy to them both. This poem really made me smile.

DAVE BILBROUGH WRITES:
I love this insightful poem. Ruth Eardley provides a poignant narrative of the transition from being in place of prominence in her community through her vocation as a trusted GP into the early stages of retirement. She observes so well the changing season that occurred for her with more time on her hands. The enforced pressures and time commitments no longer exist and for

her the challenge of adjusting to a life lived at a different pace became real.

It's interesting to see how her time and ways of connecting with people changed, and yet still with the same heart of service to others. An excellent joint winner.

ANDREW PRATT WRITES:
The narrative of this poem drew me in...Dying?... 'too young at fifty nine'... 'Now nobody wants [an opinion from] me...

So many people, and I am one, are verbs rather than nouns. I am not a thing. Like my father I am defined by what I do. And so it is for many active people, not least the GP of this poem. And all this is fine until retirement puts you away, leaves you on a shelf. Adjustment can be difficult.

A few years back I had a heart attack. During rehab we were urged to work with what was, rather than with what we wanted life to be. To do what we were able to do, not what we once did. This was mainly a physical adjustment, but it was also mental. So I identify with this GP. This is personal. A busy life. And what now?

Yet I love the way the poet adapts to what is possible and finds fulfilment in conversation or making a cup of tea. And may her life be as full now as the refreshment she offers to others. And may I, may we, reading this poem, learn its lesson over and over again as age alters and reframes our abilities and limits. Thank you for sharing, reminding me, and teaching me in this way that I may adjust to the rhythm of your verse, of my life, and be satisfied with its difference, its cadence. These words are a real gift!

ABOUT THE POET

Ruth was an NHS doctor for forty years, mostly a GP in Market Harborough, Leicestershire. A clinical tutor at Leicester Medical School, she appeared on the University's 'multi-faith panel' (where students put questions to doctors of different religions). She has a special interest in medical ethics and writes for medical magazines, devotionals and for the Christian Medical Fellowship. She also wrote a 'Dear Doctor' newspaper column for many years.

Ruth writes: "As a young teenager I remember a Physics class where we studied optics and the structure of the eye. This convinced me of two things – one, that there was no way such a complex system could have evolved (and maybe there really was a God) and two, I was going to be an eye surgeon. I later did a job in Ophthalmology which was great but I ended up in General Practice because I loved all the other specialities too! Faith in Jesus has been the bedrock of my life: it enables me to identify with people and value them. It also gives me hope because God can transform any situation: I would often pray for patients and colleagues on the way home from work."

"My poem highlights a true story – a home visit when I was supposed to be back at the surgery. I still grieve when I think of that interaction. The joy of retirement is the privilege of having time for people and being rid of ten minute appointments."

GRANDMA'S TAKEN TO SLEDDING
JENNIFER HOPE JONES (82)

May it blizzard, may it flurry
May she slip or may she slide
Grandma's taken to sledding
On HER own white-knuckle ride.

May she clatter down the hillside
May she sled until it hurts
For it is VERY chilly
When the snow gets up her skirts!

May she sled until her dentures
Rattle loudly in her head
Here's oil to the old girl's runners
Long years before she's dead,
SO
May it blizzard, may it flurry
May she slip & may she slide,
Grandma's taken to sledding
On HER own white-knuckle ride!

JUDGES' COMMENTS:

ANDREW PRATT WRITES:
This was fun from beginning to end, silly and daft, and I like that. I can be a bit daft too. At the age of seventy-five I like to challenge other people's expectations and prejudices. And that is the spirit of this poem, expressed in so few lines.

Immediately I imagine Grandma, surreptitiously creeping out before daughter or son hears the creak of the door and fears for the chill of the weather, let alone broken wrist or worse, cries of 'you really shouldn't do that at your age, granny!' Blizzard, slip, slide, white knuckle – the language races ahead of us. And I imagine the thrill of grand-children, less aware of danger, cheering Grandma on her way as they watch through the window.

What makes this a winner for me is the reality of the image. I can identify with it myself, the sense of 'you try to stop me', 'I'm not past it yet' and the reclamation of child-hood excitement in my head if not in my joints. It resonates with my experience when I first got an electric assist bike and overtook a youngster racing up a hill. It reminds me of a nonagenarian friend, to the shock horror of his adult children, taking a sky-dive for his ninetieth birthday.

May her dentures still rattle and her joy, more than childlike, live on even when the snow gets up her skirts and may she rattle on. Thanks for the joy of which this poem reminded me, and of all the fun I intend to hang onto. We are never too old for fun or joy, even if that may shock those who still wish to cosset us and protect us from our own sled-long ride! Thank you for encouraging me and bringing me joy.

ABOUT THE POET AND ARTIST

Jennifer, Jenni to her friends, was born in Reigate. She spent 35 years living and working in Worthing, Sussex, in drawing offices. She returned to Reigate in 1994 due to ill health, which amongst other symptoms took away her sight for a few short minutes. After some eye surgery it was restored, with the aid of glasses. Having been registered disabled – still retaining an active imagination, she was now free to return to her illustrations and poems of characters; enough to compile a slim collection which she has entitled, *An Illustrated Guide to Eccentrics.* Her dream is to have it published in full colour one day.

It was back in Surrey that she was awarded a place as a mature student to Epsom School of Art and Design, thus knitting together the broken threads of her art studies in 1980. Jenni writes:

"If any of my dear age compatriots, or others of all ages, have a knocking upon the door of imagination, bid them a joyful entrance."

TO YOU WHO ARE YOUNGER THAN I
ANGIE POLLARD (NEARLY 70)

I know I'm old and 'past-it',
But just stay with me a while.
I see you could be happier
And I can make you smile.

I'll share a little wisdom
Hard-earned through my mistakes,
Faults and sins and failings
Which caused my heart to break.

For life isn't always easy
When broken dreams are here,
Along with sorrow, grief and loss
And hearts so full of fear.

But after every frightening storm
There'll come a bright rainbow:
A promise that there will be joy
Is what you need to know.

It's more than just a trouble halved:
I've seen it all before.
My years have taught me many things
And that there's always more.

Joy in Ageing

For joy will come, and gladness too
To bring you much delight.
You WILL feel happiness again
Despite this endless night.

So as I see you start to smile
And gain a different view,
I'm glad for all the difficulties
That I can share with you.

It's one great joy in being old,
Advancing through the years.
I've lived so long and now I know:
That joy defeats the tears.

Age brings experience and hope
So as I share with you
My faith that joy will soon return
Is a comfort for me, too.

The giver now receives a gift
Which nothing can destroy:
That deep, deep sense of happiness –
In giving, we find joy.

DAVE BILBROUGH WRITES:

Age often does come with experience. Angie Pollard, for me hits the nail on the head by writing in her poem, To You Who are Younger Than I, words of wisdom to a younger individual. It's written in a way that we can all relate to, sharing some of the struggles, failings and challenges that life throws at us but hinting at the need for patience, perseverance and faith. Wisdom learnt from the elderly down the generations is such an important and time-honoured virtue. Finding reliable guides for life's journey who have walked ahead of us is to be valued. The old adage, 'when you learn, you teach', is so true. One of the joys of ageing is to have that privilege.

This thoughtful and accessible poem ticks all the right boxes for me.

ABOUT THE POET

Angie is 70 this year. That's an elderly person's number, not her. In her head she's in her thirties, getting younger by the day.

She's a wife; a mother of twins; a besotted grandmother of three delightful granddaughters in one family and one equally delightful grandson in the other; a teacher – still loving teaching R.E. one day a week; a coffee-loving friend. She's thankful for the years which have brought her these joys.

She's grateful for the internet which allows her to keep in close touch with family, and with friends all over the world, especially from the times she lived in Sweden and Kenya.

Loves dogs. And chocolate.

She dabbles with writing. Often a travel blog. Some little articles and stories over the years, some actually published. She loved the Embracing Age poetry challenge – finds writing to a theme is inspiring. "It's been fun reflecting on the many positives which come with living longer…"

JOY IN AGEING – HARD TO FIND
GLORIA BROWN (85)

'Joy in Ageing'? Hard to find,
Very little comes to mind.
Aches and pains and creaking knee
These for sure 'Abide with Me.'
Middle age boasts some delight
Time enough to put things right.
Lovers lost and battles won.
'Summer's lease' too quickly gone.
Now Shakespeare's seventh age of man
Tells us every sense grows 'san';
While Housman sighed for springs long spent,
And mourned the land of lost content.
Tormented Hopkins looked within
And saw a world despoiled by sin.
But then rejoiced, when spring arrived
That green miraculous growth survived.
Now Browning said 'grow old with me'
You'll find 'the best is yet to be.'
But when his dear wife thought upon it
She sighed, and penned another sonnet.
Wise Blake it was who wrote the line:
That 'joy and woe are woven fine'.
And both may come, as friend or foe,
So that is all we need to know!

(With apologies to the poets whose names I have used
and from whom I have quoted. Like Montaigne, 'I have

gathered a posy of other men's flowers, and only the thread that binds them is my own.')

PAM RHODES WRITES:

As a journalist and author of nearly 30 books, I've spent a lifetime enjoying the sheer pleasure of writing – and this poet, Gloria Brown, is my kind of girl! She certainly knows her literature, as this verse rings with the names of famous writers and familiar quotations, all woven into her own delightful poem extolling the virtues of joy. It's such an imaginative idea that she pulls off with great skill and wit. My favourite line is the postscript in which she apologises to the poets whose work she's mentioned, by quoting a line from Montaigne to explain that her verse is a 'posy of other men's flowers, and only the thread that binds them is my own'. But then, we older folk know that one of the greatest joys of ageing is that we feel free to borrow other people's good ideas and make them our own - only better!

ABOUT THE POET

Gloria lives in Beckenham. She worked as a nurse and then as a social worker in southeast London until she retired at 65.

She has a daughter and three grandchildren who live nearby. Her interests are gardening and belonging to various local groups, which include the Arts Society and RC church, and she is a keen member of her local library's book group.

This competition aroused her interest, not because she embraces old age, but because it made her think of the huge range of responses to ageing which abound in the arts. She writes,
"The poem could have been much longer but there is a limit to how many rhyming couplets one can muster up!"

A LABOUR OF LOVE

SYLVIA BROWNING (50+)

He goes out to visit the horses
Well before eight every day,
But now he uses a walking stick,
And walks with a limp all the way.

As a pink sunrise glows over the trees,
And his breath clouds the frosty air,
He trudges along with a bagful of food
For the equines in his care.

He is sometimes chased by frisky young foals
Who follow him everywhere,
Or watched by the calm, protective gaze
Of the elegant, chestnut mare.

His bright yellow bag is packed full of food -
Apples, carrots and hay-cobs too,
And he fills up the horses' water pots
With cool water, refreshing and new.

He's made many friends, with people and dogs,
Who look out for him, while on their walk,
And when they spot him, they wave from afar,
Or hurry on over, to talk.

And towards dusk, he can still be seen,
As the orange sun sets in the west

Embracing Age

Out on the field with the horses again,
Doing what he loves the best.

"I really enjoy my time with the horses,
Now that my youth has passed.
This is the place where I truly belong,
For the horses have captured my heart."

His is a Labour of Love - in action,
To feed and care for each horse,
His joy in life and his happiness
Are precious gifts -
God-given,
Of course.

A LIFE WELL LIVED
ANN CRISP (53)

A grey hair there,
a grey hair here,
growing old doesn't have to be.
Age is just a number, a clock of time,
spend your time wisely,
have fun, dance, cook, laugh with friends and be
    kindly.
Give your best, be all you can be, eat cake, don't worry
    about weight, drink copious amounts of tea.
Look to the sky,
the sun, stars and moon,
lift yourself up like an inflated balloon.
Surround yourself with animals, their comfort and
    love.
You are never alone
God is above.
Church on Sunday in Sunday dress, I do enjoy, I must
    confess.
Music is great for the soul, so is soup and a roll.
Be playful, be bold, wrap up warm in winter it gets
    cold.
Dress for comfort, not for style, stop and observe
    people for a while.
Working for charity gives clarity, it's about the giving
    not receiving.

Embracing Age

Every day is full of new joys and hope, with a bit of self
believing.

Dance in the rain, splash in the puddles, home for tea
and cat cuddles.

Take up golf, indoor or out, give that golf ball a good
old clout.

Go for a swim, or hit the gym, go to bingo and have a
big win.

Wrinkles are just like the life lines in a tree, a life well
lived is the key

Our winning photo:
Joyce celebrating her 100th birthday
with a trip to Goodwood

APPRECIATION
HOLLY TRUNDLE (57)

Joy in ageing is having time
For appreciation,
To use imagination
To draw or write some lines.

Joy in ageing is opportunity
For appreciation,
Stepping away from mechanisation
To look and revel in nature's beauty.

Joy in ageing is taking a chance
For appreciation,
Diving into education,
For the love of learning, not just to advance.

Joy in ageing is giving room,
For appreciation
Of loved friends, pets and relations,
Savouring each moment because they're gone too soon.

Joy in ageing is a blessing,
With appreciation,
And steadfast intention
To find a silver lining in everything.

Appreciative Art by Holly Trundle
Second place in the art competition

A WALK THROUGH TIME
GARY CRISP

Growing old isn't fun,
Until I remember being young,
Once upon a time, long ago.
I like once upon a times,
It's like being at the beginning of a story,
Not knowing the outcome;
A story full of wonder, adventure,
Mystery and intrigue,
A story read by someone
Who, Once upon a time,
Loved me, without doubt,
Whilst I was tucked up
Safely in my bed.
People were always friendly,
When I was young,
There weren't any arguments
Between nations,
Religions and beliefs.
Everyone was friendly,
Even the Vicars and the Priests!
As I grew older
I found it harder to talk,
Even the ministers were in a hurry,
To get back to the vicarage,
And Pray.
Everyone is busy, these days,
In their own way.

Embracing Age

My joy is remembering and
Being outdoors,
Beneath the ever changing skies,
Knowing that someone loves me,
Without doubt;
Now, the people I once loved have gone away.

I remember my dear old Grandad
Showing me the ancient gnarled, Oak trees on
      Bradgate Park,
And how his warm hands,
Held mine,
As our fingers caressed,
The deep furrows in the bark.
I remember him sitting me,
On the...
Trunk of 'Elephant Rock'
In Bradgate Park,
Part of his imagination
Became my imagination too;
And whenever I see the Rock
I wonder if other folk,
Have a similar story,
To the one that I do.

The joys of growing old,
Isn't quite the same as being young.
But I live in hope
That someone still loves me,
Without doubt,
Like the one who held me,

In my, Once upon a times.
And in the new beginnings,
Yet to come.

A Walk in Time by Gary Crisp

A WONDERFUL LIFE
SYLVIA BROWNING (50+)

"Come on in!" he said, "You're so welcome!"
And she followed him into the hall,
Where the dusk of the summer evening
Cast deep shadows onto the wall.

He shuffled ahead of her slowly,
Over a walking stick bent,
Then he opened a door
At the end of the hall,
And into the lounge they went.

His wife sat there in an armchair,
They chatted and laughed - all three,
And they asked her about
Her new job in London,
And what her future might be.

Then he told her about their garden,
And the roses he loved to grow,
And the beans he had planted
Early that year,
In neat and orderly rows.

He worked out there every morning,
He got up at half-past five,

Joy in Ageing

"It's the only way to stay young," he said,
"It really helps me survive."

And after they'd had tea and biscuits,
She said that she really must go,
It had been such a joy to call on them,
She wanted them both to know.

She waved them goodbye,
As they stood at the door,
Such a happy man, with his wife,
"Good luck!", he called out,
"God bless you, my dear,
Don't forget - It's a wonderful life!"

AGE IS A NUMBER
GWEN MOULD

I've had another birthday
The years have gone so fast.
Now suddenly I've realised
I'm getting old at last.

My hair has turned to silver
My eyes don't shine so bright.
My teeth are like the stars above
They both come out at night.

I know I must accept this
I've resigned to what's my fate.
I've come to terms that I am now
Past my sell by date.

So let's be brave and shout aloud
Don't be afraid – just yell it!
And come to terms with what you are
An old but trendy relic.

But hang on there – I've had a thought
I could also be unique.
Cos looking on the bright side
I could be called antique.

Antiques you know are ageless
Treasured – valued so they say
Rare and cherished – loved and wanted
So an old antique I'll stay.

AGEING IS JOY IN MANY FORMS
ANGELA DAVEY (59)

There's no such thing as getting old,
It's the time in our life to **enjoy** being bold,
People might say we're over the hill
But we still have hopes and **dreams to fulfil,**
We don't mind what people think
When we eat cake or enjoy a nice drink.

There's lots of adventures not to be missed -
We **get a kick** from activities, on our bucket list,
We can travel the world by boat or by plane
Or stay in a tent as it pours down with rain,
Never mind doing only what's right
We go out, have fun and do things that delight;

We're **happy** and **relish** our days of leisure
Now we've time to do things just for our own pleasure,
Nothing will stop us in our *halcyon days*
As we seek fulfilment in all kinds of ways,
Forget ageing gracefully, there's no time to rest
Get out there **have fun and live life with zest.**

BLOSSOM
CHARLIE CHURCHILL (69)

In the dancing of time, we gracefully age,
Each wrinkle a story, each line turns a page.
With the wisdom we've gained, our memories arrayed,
We find a peace that's so rich, a joy that's unswayed.

Through lines of laughter and eyes that gleam,
We embrace the journey, of a timeless theme.
With each passing year, a treasure is found,
In the quietest moments, a joy so profound.

With hearts grown tender, yet sturdy and true,
We cherish the bonds that nurtured us through.
For in the theatre of life's grand stage,
We discover such beauty that's here to assuage.

May we learn to revel in the years we have known,
To bask in the wisdom, that we call our own.
For in each chapter of life's sweet gauge,
Gleams deep essence of joy in the blossoming age.

BOTH ENDS OF THE CANDLE
SUSAN WHALLEY (67)

Youth meant shared times getting ready, giggling with
     girlfriends,
Sharing clothes, make up, Babycham and Mateus Rose
     wine.
To hit the town, to paint it red, pink, purple, whatever I
     chose!
Home in the early hours and once even when
Dawn was breaking, walking down a high street in
Evening dress, bare footed, shoes swinging in hand,
While others, sober and suited, dressed in office best
Were going to work at the start of another busy day.
Now, older, grey headed and squinting to put on
     mascara
Without my glasses, I take less time and effort,
But maybe still have a beverage to hand,
A good quality Marlborough Sauvignon Blanc.
But my enjoyment is not dimmed or diminished,
But somehow enhanced with a variety and array of
     encounters.
The company of friends, strangers, family, loved ones.
 Mamma Mia sing-along, grandson's trampoline party.
Take That concert – they've aged just as I have -
But I believe we all still look good. At least they do!
I CAN make it to the early hours, savouring every
     experience,
But truth be told, as much as I delight in activity,
I do look forward to my bed!

CAPTURING MOMENTS OF JOY
RESIDENTS OF LINTERS COURT

The gift of reliving things from the past
Sharing with other those stories that last.
The excitement of grandchildren,
    and sharing their trust
for things to come, is reward enough.
I give them my time which was once so tight,
but watching them now gives me delight.
I have the time to spend as I please,
and wear what I like to feel at ease.
To forget what I should be doing today
and fill the hours in other ways.
To do some craft or sit and knit
or read my paper for a bit.
I can relax in the shade or bask in the sun
Dreaming of the days to come,
Or an afternoon nap, followed by tea,
Balancing cake upon my knee.

Joy in Ageing

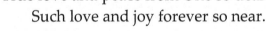

I notice the beauty in seasons much more,
and cherish those memories that went before.
I eat what I like and am grateful for choice,
and meals with others are a cause to rejoice.
I am able to settle to my favourite tv,
only to find sleep overcomes me.
I open a book, or just potter about
or get picked up and taken out.
To see old friends or phone for a chat
or prove to my family I've conquered WhatsApp.
To voice what I think is a privilege of age
And trust my outspokenness doesn't enrage.
I relish my life and all that it brings.
My faith is so dear and gives me many things,
True love and peace from One so dear
Such love and joy forever so near.

Illustrations by Sally Groves

50

CHOICES

ELIZABETH ALI (69)

My joy is such a quiet thing,
It's rather shy and retiring,
It never laughs out loud at all,
But smiles and smiles bedeck my face
At every blessing I recall
And every exploit I embrace.

"What brings this joy," I hear you ask,
It's not my mirror, that's quite clear,
Nor aches in muscles, joints, I fear,
That keep me smiling, it's the task
That may await me when I rise,
When I look out and see the skies.

Is it sunny? Walk or gardening.
Is it wet? My latest passioning.
Friends to meet, new friends to make,
Come visit me, I'll make a cake.

Now well behind me is the scourge
Of oestragen and all its moods,
(Though I am grateful for the kids),
I'm free of swings that spoil, and urge
My friends to shrug when doubt intrudes,
"Get that tattoo, no one forbids!"

Joy in Ageing

"You can't wear that!" Some may exclaim.
The woman, her of 'Purple Fame',
Is my mentor, so I will just
Say that you can 'Eat my dust!'

I won't be breaking any laws,
Or overstepping moral mores
But age has brought release from doubt
Of self, so now I try things out.
It doesn't matter if I fail,
I'll not venture beyond the pale!

A new approach to who I am,
I've turned my back on can't, I can,
May be ageing is not the key,
But certainly, it works for me.

I commend it to you.

COUNT YOUR BLESSINGS
JUNE HUGHES (81)

Joy, Oh what joy when you get a letter
To see a specialist to make you better

Old age doesn't always bring good news
But grandchildren and outings help to chase the blues

Looking for joy in simple ordinary everyday things
Like spotting a ladybird or butterfly wings

Joy is reminiscing hearing a favourite tune
or peeping through the curtains at a full moon

Growing old together renewing your vows
Just sitting quietly whiling away the hours

What pleasure to receive a letter or card
And then manage to walk a hundred yards

So to sum up all these wonderful things
There is joy in what every old age brings

JOY IN AGEING: DELIGHT
ELIZABETH ALI (69)

What could this phrase for us imply?
A miriad fancies dancing by.
On which will our attention lie?
'Delightfulness' might clarify!

Delight in time that is our own
To do and be, our skill sets hone,
Walk till we're tired to the bone
And spend forever on the phone!

To know we can be useful too,
A bank, as needed, for our crew,
Hard graft in earlier years now through,
We are in charge of what we do,
(God willing, as long as we can be.)

Delight in simply being you,
Learn to love, - others love you too,
Rejoice in everything you do,
Seek only for the good and true.

Enjoying and supporting friends,
Sharing love that never ends,
Ceasing to be she who pretends,
'Embracing ageing' comprehends.

EMBRACING GETTING OLDER
KATHY WALLER (75)

My last day at work and I finally feel free
No more alarms or early morning for me
I am retiring, but I really don't feel old
Enjoy yourself, relax, life begins now I've been told.

The first few years went like a dream
I planned so much, I went to the extreme
What jobs I would finish, and the places I'd go
Family to visit, Friends and people I know.

But time doesn't stop when you retire
Looking back I seem to have lost the desire
To do all the things that I wanted to do
But I still fitted in quite a few.

My body said slow down, you're not young anymore
It takes me time just to answer the door
My Heart and Brain say's you're not all that old
So take your time, and do as you're told.

Join a group or a club and go once a week
For a chat, have lunch or just sit and speak
Remembering things we can share together
From family and pets to the food and the weather.

Taking time for myself, I slowed down and have fun
Embracing the years and the person I've become
I now have more friends than I had before
Its club day, I'm okay, I can't write anymore.

55

FINDING JOY
ANGIE POLLARD (NEARLY 70)

I may not have the legs of youth
Or arms to hold you tight.
Yet joy in seeing you will cause
My smiles to be as bright.

I might not hear you quite as well
Or see your lovely face,
Yet when we are together, we
Find joy in our safe place.

You may not realise the gift
Your visits give to me
Yet one day you will recognise
That giving is the key.

We give each other gifts of time,
heart talks and cups of tea.
And as we share the things we love
We receive the gift of glee.

Find pleasure in togetherness
in every word delight.
Our company will bring us joy,
Let's hold on – with all our might.

For feeble legs or arms won't work,
But smiles and laughter do.
So Joy will be our closest friend -
My prayer for me and you.

FIND WHAT YOU LOVE TODAY
TERENCE FOSTER (73)

Find what you love today,
A well-tried place or somewhere new?
 Choices galore are waiting for you.

Love what you find today
Fresh air strolls or bright sunny heat?
Choosing with care creates a new treat.

Everyday choices, like stepping stone ways,
Pay with interest what searching conveys.

Wish what you want today,
Taking more time to clear each thought
When outlooks form using faith we're taught.

Want what you wish today,
Time to go slow, no rush or speed,
 Haste adds nothing but sad restless need.

Everyday choices, like stepping stone ways,
Pay with interest what calmness conveys.

Sure to be pleased today
Smiles show signs that aims are content,
So in your heart hold safe what is meant.

Joy in Ageing

Pleased to be sure today
Old friends or new, saving the best,
To keep dear bonds that show we are blessed.

Everyday choices, like stepping stone ways,
Pay with interest what friendship conveys.

Love what you hear today.
Each season's sounds still frame fond scenes,
Then changes mark time, and all that means.

Hear what you love today.
Uplifting notes from fine-tuned strings
Lighten low times, with great joys that brings.

Everyday choices, liking stepping stone ways,
Pay with interest what music conveys.

So which things count most today?
Joys we now have, kept in our hearts,
Or untried steps that bring us fresh starts?
Tomorrow's just another day, they say,
So really enjoy all we have, today.

FIT FOR PURPOSE

ROSALIE GROTTICK (82)

70 years is the age to attain,
Then each added year is a time that's been gained.
So the 80 plus years that I have now lived,
Have they been fit for purpose,
Or was there more I could give?
Some times have been easy,
And I've felt really blessed
But some have been hard,
And I have to confess,
That I've not always coped in the way that I might.
And have walked in the dark,
Instead of Christ's light.
But I want you to know, as long as I live
That to you, my dear Jesus
All my love do I give.

GRANDCHILDREN
MICHAEL JACKSON (73)

Children may be the arrows of our adulthood,
So that we celebrate our quiver-full with pride,
But we little imagine the path beyond our
Shared engagement with life's troughs and triumphs.

As that path overshadows with stooping branches,
Creaking echoes of limbs outworn and tired,
A parting opens in life's thicket with rays of
Focussed sunshine, dancing with new beginnings.

Joy is all the more sweet for its cherished surprise
At new arrows, resting in our children's quivers.
Nobody foretold quite how disarming would be
This unexpected advent, a new generation of hope.

Just as each child's arrival blessed a little more,
Now in my old age those blessings multiply.
But the marvelled mystery which swells my heart
Is celebrating each grandchild's distinctness.

Inexpressible and glorious are the emotions
Which engage my heart and mind, as mouth I must
Thanks to Him for unexpected depth of delight
That crowns my waning years with such fruition.

Watching new young lives embrace the present
Sheds of joy of peace on my foreshortened future,
And in this I find acceptance of my journey's past;
These lives are undreamt gift and treasured balm.

HAPPINESS
(My mathematical model for how this increases with age)
MATTHEW SUMNER (50+)

I've estimated the number of rings in my cherry tree
As at the end of December 2023

And then for mathematical rigour
I've taken the **log** of the square **root** of this figure

The higher my age compared to this calculation
The greater my level of relaxation

The older I get the happier I must be
Although these sums do **sap** my energy

I'm sure that once you've **leaf**ed through the data
You'll agree with my theory sooner or later

And furthermore my cherry tree adds to the good
    cheer
With its beautiful blossom year after year

HAVE YOU NOT HEARD
PAMELA FERGUSON (72)

I will renew you
as in the springtime of childhood
your spirit soared
and you saw imagined worlds
where the skies knew no bounds.
With the wings of a bird
you followed your heart
knowing you were loved.

I will restore you
as in the summer of youth
you ran, focused, swift and free
on field and track and alleyway,
hearing the voice of hope,
word of life for your soul,
finding healing in broken places.
When you fell, I lifted you.

I will replenish you
as in fruitful autumn days–
gifts of grace beyond measure,
and when winter closes in
and the ground is unsteady beneath your feet
I am with you still.
Take each step, each breath with me.
You are strong as I hold you.

Embracing Age

Do you not know, have you not heard?
I am the Creator,
you've tasted the bounty of the earth.
We'll walk together and not faint.

Come, weary and burdened,
you will find rest
for I am gentle and humble in heart.
You will dance with joy in your soul.

JENNY'S JOY
BRENDAN CONBOY (63)

Has she passed her warranty, heading for obscurity?
She clutches her security, the joy of her maturity.
Her memories replace her sight
Fill her heart with such delight
Though she is slight, she's still a might
But cannot do the things she'd like

Memories of bombs and eating rations
Her garden is still her life-long passion
Blooming snowdrops bring such joy
Memories of meeting a boy
She laughed and loved in the shrubbery
Life's journey of joy and discovery

She gathered much erudition and wisdom
Joyfully shared, knowledge given
Even when her joy was hidden
She relaxes with her knitting needles
Despite her age and feeling feeble
Joyfully teaches younger people

Everyday ushers in a treat
She's filled with joy with every greet
Her joy affects the ones she meets
Her countenance is contagious
Joyful and courageous
Still, remaining gracious

64

JOB'S COMFORTERS!
JULIE JORDAN (70)

What's the joy in ageing?
I asked three friends one day.
There really isn't anything
That's joyful, they all say.

One says that both her knees are bad,
One hates her sagging skin.
Another says her back goes out
More than a wheelie bin.

I try to say they all look great,
But you know that I'd be lying.
They're not laughter lines – they're wrinkles,
And they needed a darned good iron!

They reminisce on days gone by
Of times spent in their youth.
But now don't feel like having fun,
Saying they're too long in the tooth.

Long in the tooth? I say to them.
We're lucky we don't yet have dentures.
We're still young at heart and free
To go on fabulous wild adventures!

Our get up and go has got up and gone
We've no need to be super fit.

Joy in Ageing

We just want to lead the quiet life
To read, watch TV or knit.

Oh, come on ladies, I say to them.
We've got so much life still to live.
After all it's got to be
Better than the alternative.

Why don't you join me for a walk?
Come now, there's no need to scoff.
Oh dear, this conversation is pointless,
As all three have just nodded off!

I do like to exercise each day,
All that stretching does me good.
For you see, I know I'm doing well
When I reach out and don't touch wood!

JOY IN AGEING!
JUDITH GREEN

All things bright and beautiful,
All creatures great and small
Some worn round the edges
The Lord God made them all.

Each morning eye that opens
Each knee cap's creaking twinge.
When sunrise shows our wrinkles
It's lemon in the gin.

All things bright and beautiful,
This octave is too high,
Let's drop to something lower
Or let the words go by.

All things bright and beautiful
All old ones great and small,
We'll toast another morning,
Lord help us, one and all.

JOY IN JESUS
JULIE JORDAN

J esus my precious Saviour and King
O pen my mouth, give me a new song to sing
Y ou deserve all the praise I can bring.

I n joyous harmony I'll sing with You
N ever ending hope, You make all things new

A melody of love to You is due.
G rateful for keeping me through the years
E ven ones filled with sorrow and fears
I long for the day when my dear Lord appears
N earer to You and Your wonderful face
G oing Homewards to my Saviour's embrace.

JOY OF THE LORD
LOIS WILTSHIRE

Joy of the Lord is ours each day,
A Joy that encourages us on our way,
It comes with Faith and Hope and Love,
Joy comes with wings to look above.

J stands for Jesus, the light of my life,
With my husband in Heaven, I'm no longer a wife,
With Jesus, my Saviour, I'm not on my own,
Even though now I live all alone.

O is for others, both family and friends,
And others I meet before the day ends,
They might be lonely, I'll give them a smile,
And maybe share our time for a while.

Y is for You, whoever you be,
May you know this Joy, given so free,
Yes, Joy is a gift, from Jesus, your Friend,
A Joy that can never, never end.

The Joy of Jesus helps us on our way,
And whatever life throws at us each day,
As we grow older, the days seems so long,
But the Joy of Jesus will be our song.

Joy in Ageing

So 'Joy in Ageing' is reality,
Is daily available to you and me,
And in the night when we cannot sleep,
Let us focus on Jesus, not count the sheep!

This life, like a tunnel – when will it end?
It goes up and down and round many a bend,
It will take me to Heaven, at last, one day,
With my Joy complete, "Thank you Jesus, I'll say".

KEEP ME PLODDING, LORD
(An Old Woman's Prayer)
JEAN WYATT (88)

'Those who hope in the Lord will renew their strength.
They will soar on wings like eagles;
they will run and not grow weary,
they will walk and not be faint.'
Your promise, Lord; a password used for years: I s a
    40,31, reminding me.

To rise, rise, rise, and, God-like, gaze down from on
    high,
to view the distant scene with wide, discerning eye,
to soar above the mess,
    (then pounce upon a poor wee mouse I guess.)
But no, the pouncing's not the promised thing.
    Just look — the rise, the lift,
        the soar, the drift,
            the hover, the float; and the view!
            How I wish!!
But— so remote, so distant,
    so unlikely, so very high.

Perhaps I could ask for seagull's flight.
    They too soar and drift on a breeze,
        on the air; on the *ruah-breath of the wind.
(Then they squawk and they fight; beg for food with no
    shame)
    — but they're here. They are near.

Joy in Ageing

More homely, more possible.
And a seagull today was a beautiful thing,
An arrow of silver, turned on a wing,
flung a promise, a hope, of a rising to sing —
Maybe a seagull will do.

But please Lord —keep me walking, walking —
'To walk and not feint.' I'll settle for that.
Keep me walking Lord.
Or — plodding. Just plodding will do.
Yes, I'll plead for one thing: keep me plodding
a while yet.
One day will be the end, I know — But not yet, not yet
—

There are things I hope to do.
Stories I hope to write,
Thoughts I hope to sift.
Keep me plodding a while yet.

And I wait, Lord, I wait for You — Gaze… Praise…
for those soaring -Seagull-or-Eagle *ruah-flights
that give me a song.

*Ruah = Hebrew for wind, spirit, breath (Genesis 1:2
etc)

MEDITATION ON JOY
ELIZABETH ALI (69)

Joy is a learned thing.
You want to be joyful?
Learn from the best!

Where did we start?
Look at a young baby.
By six weeks they have learnt to smile.
It's a smile that fills our hearts with joy.
That baby knows the joy too.
Can you imagine how he feels?
He gazes up and recognises
For the first time,
The configuration of the one
That always comes to his call.
You knew that once too.
The realisation of the value
Of a responsive human face.

By the time we are old,
(No definition offered),
Perhaps we can learn
 To smile with joy again
At the sight of a human face?

The thrill of being loved and loving,
Giving, and receiving, care,
Gratitude within our souls

Joy in Ageing

For every opportunity,
To share, or to accept, a blessing.
These are food and drink to joy.

Like with the butterfly,
Don't try to catch joy.
Sit quietly in some lovely sunny dale.
Breathe gently and wait patiently
And it will come to you
And settle on the fragrant flower
That blooms within your heart.

MEMORIES
PEGGY APPLEYARD (93)

Memory is a funny thing,
It lets you down with age.
A name you have known all your life
Is wiped clean from the page.
No matter how you try to think
And rack your poor old brain.
It just won't come, then in a flash,
You remember it again.

       I sometimes can't remember
       What I had for tea last night.
       Yet a bag of chips when I was young
       I remember every bite.
       Don't know the names of songs now,
       Though I hear them every day.
       But I can still sing all the words
       Of songs we used to play.

I've only got to smell wood smoke
And I'm transported back,
To happy days of camping,
With the boisterous Youth club pack.
There are such happy memories
Of things we used to do.
I know I'll not forget them
Hope they'll recall me too.

Joy in Ageing

Yes memory is a strange thing
It can be quite a pain.
But it's nice to know that with its help,
We relive things again.

Another winning photo of Joyce celebrating her 100th
birthday – this time sailing.

MEMORIES
GWEN MOULD

Memories are precious
Stored forever in our mind.
A snapshot of occasion
A fleeting gift in time.

Memories are precious
Of schooldays fun and laughter.
Of holidays and birthdays
Of children's happy ever after.

Memories are precious
Though sometimes sad with pain
Until a grandchild's words of love
Can make you smile again.

Memories are precious
Growing older – finding love.
Watch your babies grow and prosper
Watched we hope by God above.

Memories are precious
Even more as we grow old.
A lifetime stored – remembered
Is worth its weight in gold.

NOW IS THE TIME
ANN MILTON (62)

I've never had the time for joy
just one more thing on
the never-ending to do list.
Happiness I could manage, it was pleasing
and easy to combine with work and the school run.

But joy I realise now is not something to do but a way
      to be,
a choice that I am finally able to embrace.
It is sheathes of coloured silk, engulfing me
giving life to my weary body, whilst
arousing my senses all over.

Confident in its riches I throw open the door;
lay aside the happy but joyless years.
Done with the duties that seemed to define me
at last I can realise, with courage and joy,
the fruit of my own long cherished dreams.

OH GREAT AUNT!
JENNIFER HOPE-JONES (82)

The Great Aunt of Seventy three
Shamelessly climbed up a tree
The reason my dear
Was not very clear
But her Nephew yelled, "On"
With great glee.

She tottered the length
Of the bough
While juggling with cherries
Some how...

But could not keep up
On both feet
So her fall was; rapid
But neat

While her Nephew loudly approved
Oh Aunt, Please,
PLEASE, do it again
For a treat!

ON GROWING OLD JOYFULLY
JOAN (91)

Now is the time to dry those tears
And just be glad for all the years
Life well lived is truly joyful
Even though at times it's painful

Teeth fall out, our hair as well
Bunions grow and ankles swell
The eyes grow dim, we cannot hear
A catalogue of woes I fear

Mirrors show some extra wrinkles
And, dare I say, there's night time tinkles
Yet not all is doom and gloom
In fact, there is still time to bloom

Now's the time to search your memory
I'm sure its loss is only temporary!
Remember happy family times
Reciting all those nursery rhymes?

Whilst we long for yesteryear
When little ones were in our care
The years have blessed us more and more
You'd never guess we've reached fourscore.

OUT OF OFFICE
ANGUS JOHNSON (62)

45 years! from student apprentice to senior manager,
Problems to solve, people to meet, conference speaker,
I cherished my personal seat in the office,
Promotions, awards, colleagues, progress!

Then the boss said, " You are a man of virtue, we
    admire,
But it's time to stop - please go home, you must retire!
Now I sit solidly on my bum, until it's numb,
Sing songs, forgotten the words, so, just hum!

Each day my eyes intently gaze ahead,
I certainly ensure my body is well fed,
In the same seated position hour after hour,
My feet rotate and provide the power!

I may kind of be sitting around and still,
But I've just cycled up another hill,
I realise my past office views were myopic,
Sights from this summit are kaleidoscopic!

Grass, yellow rape, green leafed trees, a glistening
    river,
A steam train passing through the valley gives me a
    shiver,
Black cattle, spotted pigs, white woolly sheep,
Breathe in the beauty - I have a quiet weep!

Exploring the outdoor world has awaken me,
The design, intricacy, and interwoven activity.
The extraordinary, amazing creation!
God be praised. Total appreciation!

Cyclists After Elevenses by Angus Johnson

SALSA DANCING
SYLVIA BROWNING (50+)

Salsa dancing - Salsa Passion
Early springtime weather,
Count the rhythm,
Learn the first steps,
Back, Replace, Together.

Coloured lights move silently,
In soft, concentric circles,
All around us, everywhere -
Bright blue, red, pink and purple.

The atmosphere is wonderful -
Romantic, tinged with sadness,
But Salsa dancing fills the heart
Again, with hope and gladness.

Making new friends, having fun,
Sharing joy and laughter,
Learning moves from everyone -
Fresh tips from different partners.

Learn to do the Open Hold,
Cross-body, Change of Place,
And, later on, the New York Walk,
With elegance and grace.

Embracing Age

Salsa dancing - Love the music,
And the joyful rhythm
Is like a summer holiday,
Beneath a starry heaven.

Picture a secluded beach,
Where small waves shine and shimmer,
Reflecting the pearlescent light
Of the moon's soft glimmer.

Salsa dancing - Joy in movement
Bringing us together,
The love of dance, at any time,
Will surely last for ever.

TESTING THE WATERS
ROSALIE GROTTICK (82)

Sarah gave birth to a son at age 90
As promised by the Lord.
Countless promises to you and me,
Are recorded in God's word.

At the great age of 80 God chose Moses,
To bring Israel to the promised land.
You and I have also been chosen.
To reveal the Saviours hand.

85 year old Caleb had a hard task ahead,
To conquer the land of the giants.
Our task might need us a hard road to tread
To defeat our spiritual tyrants.

Many saints of all ages throughout the years
Have succeeded against the odds.
Experiencing joy and facing fears
With the strength which comes from God.

So let us step out of our comfort zone
Let us test the untried waters.
Knowing God will never leave us alone.
His arms are there to support us.

THE ARTIST
JUDITH GREEN

They dance in the moonlight
the sea is their waltz, small waves their orchestra
hushing the night to nothing but them
absorbed in each other
like stars hold the sky.

On the edge of the sand,
she sits in the summer night,
gin and tonic in hand, recalling the picture,
painting her memories
when she danced, joyous in moonlight…
and raises her glass.

Dancing by Patricia Jeal, aged 86

Joy in Ageing

THE BEST IS YET TO COME
ROSALIE GROTTICK (82)

It's no fun getting old,
Is a phrase I have often heard.
What with aches and pains and feeling cold,
Eyes growing dim, and I can't hear a word.

But let's not forget what has gone before,
When we were young, without a care,
When cleaning the house didn't seem like a chore.
And the days ahead seemed set to fair.

What of the present? We are not finished yet.
So pick yourself up and dust yourself down.
Put on your glad rags and get your hair set,
Call up your friends and hit the town.

Our days happily busy doing just as we please,
With no tight agenda or alarm to set.
Plenty of time for afternoon teas.
And if we are late home no one will fret.

Now we look forward with great anticipation,
Knowing the best is yet to come.
Through Jesus Christ, the way of our salvation,
We will be with Him in our eternal home.

THE BUTTON JAR
MONKSCROFT POETRY CLUB

The variety of buttons you see in that jar -
each one has a story to tell -
each one from a garment, some we've forgotten
but some we remember them well:

Liberty bodices that kept us warm -
remember the buttons they had?
They were rubber and fiddly because they were small,
not designed for young fingers at all!

Tipped from the jar like a glistening shoal
what seemed like a handful at first
are a rainbow of buttons spread out on a tray
and one of the poets starts to relate
Laurie Lee's story about winter's cold
when all of the children were sewn into their clothes
and to make the smell worse, just before that,
their chests were rubbed over with 'protective' goose
    fat!

We remember our favourite buttons,
one from the Order of St John,
someone else can still see the slippers she had
with ladybirds on.
One poet has tortoiseshell buttons
or as she said, they are like tabby cats

Joy in Ageing

another wears all mismatched buttons
she likes them like that!

What could we do with the buttons
apart from use them on clothes?

We could make necklaces, bracelets and bookmarks,
cards with floral designs like a rose.

So thank you the lady who brought them
they have brightened our poetry day
here is the poem we've sewn
with the thread of our memories today.

THE ENGLISH OAK
JULIE JORDAN

They say from little acorns
Mighty oak trees grow.
One little seed germinates,
Buried in the rich soil below.

I was born one wonderful Autumn,
A little sapling, then a tree.
You were not there at my birth,
Nor my dying days will see.

As I continue to grow tall and strong,
Deep in the ancient wood.
My smooth bark and spreading branches
Mature to adulthood.

They say it takes 300 years.
To grow, the same to live.
Even in my dying days,
I know I still have much to give.

There's a joy in getting older,
Recalling the seasons I've seen.
Dressed in gold and brown for autumn,
From barren again to green.

My bark matures and thickens,
Becoming rugged and rough.

91

Joy in Ageing

Fungi and lichen cling to me,
Acorns grow plump and tough.

My canopy is a shelter.
For squirrels, bats and birds.
More than 2000 species are
Supported by me, so I've heard.

Boys have climbed, lovers have kissed.
Initials carved in my trunk.
They say pixies wear the acorn caps,
From the cupules fairies have drunk.

It's a joy when the various little birds
Build their nests in my outstretched arms.
They know they are safe and sheltered,
And I won't let them come to harm.

The seasons continue to come and go,
But oh, what a life I have led.
Now another acorn will fall to the ground.
And take my place when I'm dead.

THE JOY OF GRANDCHILDREN
PAULINE KENNINGTON (65)

I'm what you might call self-sufficient
And at caring for me most proficient
With a cat on my knee
And a nice cup of tea
Seems there's nothing of which I'm deficient
To romancing I'm now quite resistant
With no suitors at present persistent
I work best on my own
Like a queen on her throne
With romantic intentions far distant
To my critics I'm rarely compliant
My track-record is being defiant
I've spent too many years
Wasted too many tears
Feeling harassed and too acquiescent
I'm not quite the lady omniscient
But at gathering gossip consistent
It's not just that I'm curious
But it does seem more spurious
To impart news that proves inefficient
My children have moved on insistent
That I'll make it because I'm belligerent
But how little they know
Just how slow time can go
When close mingling is so intermittent
Too many old friendships have gone
As time passes and people move on

Joy in Ageing

So I'm counting my blessings
And learning new lessons
Until ageing is finally done
For a catch up please make an appointment
In a bid to avoid disappointment
When you visit you'll see
That I'm still the old me
Ageing nicely with gracious contentment

Photo by Susan Whalley: With the Grandchildren

THE JOY OF LIFE
GILL BRADBURY (76)

The joy of life is music
since a lullaby surrounds
the baby in its cradle
with earliest, distant sounds.

Enjoyed with infant friendships
in the playground and the streets,
those simple rhymes of childhood
our happiness now completes.

Then in the swinging sixties,
that's when Elvis was the King,
we danced away the hours.
Rock and roll the hottest thing!

Through our lives we listened more,
our teenage tastes expanded.
A whole range of music genres
became what we demanded.

Along this life time's journey
while we danced and played and sang,
the music just got sweeter
as through all our lives it rang.

And in my maturer years
it is now the greatest thrill

accessing tunes from way back
that are my favourites still.

While the years move on apace
it gives me so much pleasure
to know the music never fades;
its sounds go on forever.

Third place in our multimedia
competition – Grandad Gaming

TITHONUS
WILLIAM BARNETT

Trembling lady, young in old, I shall be
Your Tithonus at peace; my prudent sell-by date
Courtesy of Christ Jesus, His gift of life to me.
Immortality is on hold; trusting, we shall wait.

Chariot me through portent clouds, cerise in flow,
Let me be your caring clown and ever beguiled;
No sad slough of despond can sap our fervent glow
For I felt safe and secure when you first smiled.

I laugh and I'm so loved as you arise,
Goddess of the dawn and every precious hour;
All that I am is held within your perfect eyes,
Suffused, I breathe your every passing flower.

We are sublimed in prayer when shadows fall,
Life is short and time comes down to this:
We're safely gathered in and we are enthralled,

We say yet more in a breathless hug and a cocoa kiss.

TREASURE HUNT

ANGIE POLLARD (NEARLY 70)

An unexpected sunset;
a rainbow after rain;
that cheery, kindly phone call:
and I find Joy again.

She lingers next my bedside
smiling lovingly at me.
She taps a greeting on the door:
I welcome her with glee.

She's in every happy meeting,
in a letter, call or card.
She whispers, "Here I am, choose ME –
it's really not that hard."

I'll keep my eyes wide open,
my heart and thinking too.
I'll find Joy in just ANYTHING -
It can't be hard to do.

For Joy is my companion
As I journey ever on.
My friend in every twist and turn –
My life is SO MUCH FUN!

WARNING
PAMELA-MARIE LUMBROSO (67)

Do not hide in "beige", or "taupe" or "cream".
Sallow boring colours that have not the right to bear
    the name 'colour'.
They will weigh you down, silence your voice, make
    heavy your steps.
Until you become a faceless, voiceless, shadow.
That no one notices, until they trip over you, and you
    are the one that says 'sorry'!

Do not settle for "fawn", or "buff "or "oatmeal."
It will act like an eraser and slowly rub you out,
Until you are a- thin sheet of tracing paper- person.

Do not wear "camel", or "ecru" or "stone".
Regardless of what the magazines will tell you.
And please do not wear the opinions of others!
Because if left unchecked, they will totally erode away
    any hint of joy or daring or revolution you once
    had.

The antidote is colour, dazzling, bright, mixed together
    or on its own.
Red, blue, green, orange, yellow, purple, pink.
Paisley, checks, spots, dots and squiggles and splashes!
And not just your clothes, but on your hair and
    everywhere.

And, after the first application, you will see immediate
  results.
No longer invisible, faceless or voiceless. No longer a
  shadow.
But MAGNIFICENT, in glorious technicolour!

WHAT IS JOY?
TRACEY TREGENNA (62)

Joy, is it that thing
which keeps us steady?
Is it an extension of how
or what we want to be
In our later years?
If I could harness it
I would embrace it.
Yet so often it slips from my hands.
Joy is deep, it's found in simple pleasures
When I connect with you Lord.
That is Joy.
It's not really about age.
For inside, I still feel that
better days are to come.
Much like I felt in my youth
We halt our own joy by poor choices
Joy is not a passing emotion,
but something much more.
It's a completeness.
So as I find myself in you God
My family and friends
I try to hold on to it
These last simmerings of life
I want more bubble in.
Reckless bubbles.
Like your love for us dear Lord.
Until then, I will keep searching

within myself.
So as to connect with you fully
In this time, may I learn to be kind
Have the grace of old age
to learn from another.
Often another, much younger than me
So Joy my friend, can be found
in mature years.
But let me be childlike enough
to sit and know your way
dear Lord.

WHEN I RETIRED
SUE WHITEFORD (73)

When I retired, I vowed that I would:

1. Spend at least one day just reading, all the books I haven't had time to read; and maybe even re-read those that I enjoyed.

2. Take a cup of tea back to bed and listen to the radio in tranquil peace, something that I couldn't do when I was employed.

3. Learn Calligraphy, oh I would love to write so beautifully, then create my own cards and write a lovely verse within.

4. Or maybe start my own home-brewing, how much cheaper would it be if I could make "Sue's Homemade Gin".

5. Join a walking club to stay keeping fit and well, with waterproof coat, sticks and boots, I would really look the part.

6. I'll look after the grandchildren and we will run and we'll play 'cos I'm really still young at heart!

So here I am 12 years on -

1. A lot of the books that I haven't yet read, are still stuck on the shelf.

2. I get a headache if I lie long in bed, it's clearly not good for my health!

3. And with Arthritis in my hands, well I just can't win!

4. And as for starting homebrew, well I really don't like Gin!

5. I've got a bus pass and a car on the drive and if it's raining, well I'm afraid, that's that!

6. Grandchildren, well they're all at school now and busy with clubs after that!

So I'm :

- Chatting with friends, cinemas, lunch out and coach trips, as a pensioner I get the odd perk.

- But one thing that I query now, is - How on earth did I find time to go out to work!!

YOU'LL HAVE JOY
RICHARD COOK (72)

I've left my youth so far behind,
And now I've ceased the daily grind,
Although my face has become lined,
There's joy in ageing I find.

"What joy?" you may ask as you creak
"Surely the outlook is just bleak!
My strength has gone and I feel weak,
Where is this joy of which you speak?"

'There's joy in children and friends,
How much you want, it all depends;
While following the peaceful trends
You will find the joy never ends.'

'Then whether a girl or boy,
Grandchildren will provide more joy.
They learn such things, it's not a ploy,
With the hope and love you employ.'

'So look forward to each new day,
Put aches and pains out of the way.
Keep your mind sharp with laughs and play,
Then you'll have joy that's here to stay!'

Joy in Ageing

YOU'RE ONLY AS OLD AS YOU FEEL
PAMELA-MARIE LUMBROSO (67)

Eat that cake, wear that scarf,
Read a joke, have a laugh.
You're only as old as you feel.

Get a tattoo if you dare!
Buy some cheeky underwear.
You're only as old as you feel.

Take some classes or learn to swim.
You've still got some vigour and vim.
 You're only as old as you feel.

Learn to dance, or learn to box.
Try something different with your locks.
You're only as old as you feel.

Play hopscotch if you're able.
Use your best China on the table.
You're only as old as you feel.

Book that trip! Buy those tickets,
Yes, eat your favourite biscuits.
You're only as old as you feel.

What I'm really trying to say
Is have a go, do it today coz,
You're only as old as you feel!

ACKNOWLEDGEMENTS

Having dabbled our toes in poetry competitions and book publishing for the first time last year, we were feeling buoyant. Let's include art and multi-media as well as poetry this year we chimed confidently! Had we thought it through a bit more carefully, it might have dawned on us that three competitions in one means three times the amount of work! So deadlines loomed precariously as the team tried to bring it altogether.

And what a team effort it's been. A huge thank you to Pam Harrison, Roz de Lord and Liz Windaybank, our wonderful volunteers at Embracing Age who have had their tech skills stretched as they scanned, filed and logged all the entries, read through all the poems and helped to shortlist, and judged the multimedia entries. They have been the stars of the show, beavering away in the background. Of course, we couldn't have a competition without judges and we are hugely grateful to Pam Rhodes, Dave Bilbrough and Andrew Pratt for judging the poetry, and to Paul Hobbs, Roger Wagner and Karina Phillips for judging the art work. And a special word of appreciation to Pam Rhodes who wrote the foreword for this book and featured the winning poems on her radio show, "Hearts and Hymns". Thank you for all your enthusiasm and encouragement.

A special shout out to Holly Trundle for being so willing to proof read the final draft. Thank you.

And finally, thank you to everyone who submitted poems, art work and multi media to the competition. Thank you for harnessing your creativity and joining us in this contribution towards rewriting the narrative on ageing. Let's continue to voice our belief that ageing isn't all doom and gloom, rather it is filled with hope, with joy and with... (you'll have to wait and see what the theme of next years competition will be!)

Tina English

Founder of Embracing Age

ABOUT EMBRACING AGE

We're a Christian charity that's all about older people. We want to encourage a positive view of getting older, hence our themes of hope and joy in ageing. We want our communities and our churches to be great places to grow old.

We're working towards a world where older people are valued, respected and full of hope. We recognise that sometimes in our advancing years frailty can develop, causing us to be more dependent than perhaps we would like. But physical and cognitive decline don't diminish our worth, and we are determined to embrace those journeying through frailty with love, kindness and dignity.

We have three main strands to our work: befriending care home residents, supporting informal carers and equipping churches in their work with older people. If you want to find out more, please visit our website or contact us:

embracingage.org.uk
info@embracingage.org.uk

Printed in Great Britain
by Amazon

47939786R10066